Moses the Kitten
James Herriot

Illustrated by Peter Barrett

Michael Joseph/Adam & Charles Black

There have been times in the winter when I have regretted being a vet and this looked like one of them.

I had driven about ten miles from home, thinking all the time that the Dales always looked their coldest, not when they were covered with snow, but as now, when the first sprinkling streaked the bare flanks of the fells in bars of black and white like the ribs of a crouching beast. And now in front of me was a farm gate rattling on its hinges as the wind shook it.

The car, heaterless and draughty as it was, seemed like a haven in an uncharitable world and I gripped the wheel tightly with my woollen-gloved hands for a few moments before opening the door. The wind almost tore the handle from my fingers as I got out but I managed to crash the door shut before stumbling over the frozen mud to the gate. Muffled as I was in heavy coat and scarf pulled up to my ears I could feel the icy gusts biting at my face, whipping up my nose and hammering painfully into the air spaces in my head.

I had driven through and, streaming-eyed, was about to get back into the car when I noticed something unusual. There was a frozen pond just off the path and among the rime-covered rushes which fringed the dead opacity of the surface a small object stood out, shiny black.

I went over and looked closer. It was a tiny kitten, probably about six weeks old, huddled and immobile, eyes tightly closed. Bending down, I poked gently at the furry body. It must be dead; a morsel like this couldn't possibly survive in such cold . . . but no, there was a spark of life because the mouth opened soundlessly for a second then closed.

Quickly I lifted the little creature and tucked it inside my coat. As I drove into the farmyard I called to the farmer who was carrying two buckets out of the calf house. "I've got one of your kittens here, Mr Butler. It must have strayed outside."

Mr Butler put down his buckets and looked blank. *"Kitten?* We haven't got no kittens at present."

I showed him my find and he looked more puzzled.

"Well that's a rum 'un, there's no black cats on this spot. We've all sorts o' colours but no black 'uns."

"Well he must have come from somewhere else," I said. "Though I can't imagine anything so small travelling very far. It's rather mysterious."

I held the kitten out and he engulfed it with his big, work-roughened hand.
''Poor little beggar, he's only just alive.
I'll take him into t'house and see if the missus can do owt for him.''

In the farm kitchen Mrs Butler was all concern. "Oh what a shame!" She smoothed back the bedraggled hair with one finger. "And it's got such a pretty face." She looked up at me. "What is it, anyway, a him or a her?"

I took a quick look behind the hind legs. "It's a Tom."

"Right," she said. "I'll get some warm milk into him but first of all we'll give him the old cure."

She went over to the fireside oven on the big black kitchen range, opened the door and popped him inside.

I smiled. It was the classical procedure when new-born lambs were found suffering from cold and exposure; into the oven they went and the results were often dramatic. Mrs Butler left the door partly open and I could just see the little black figure inside; he didn't seem to care much what was happening to him.

The next hour I spent in the byre wrestling with the hind feet of a cow. The cleats were overgrown and grossly misshapen and upturned, causing the animal to hobble along on her heels. My job was to pare and hack away the excess horn and my long held opinion that the hind feet of a cow were never meant to be handled by man was thoroughly confirmed. We had a rope round the hock and the leg pulled up over a beam in the roof but the leg still pistoned back and forth while I hung on till my teeth rattled. By the time I had finished the sweat was running into my eyes and I had quite forgotten the cold day outside.

S till, I thought, as I eased the kinks from my spine
when I had finished, there were compensations.
There was a satisfaction in the sight of the cow
standing comfortably on two almost normal
looking feet.

"Well that's summat like," Mr Butler grunted.
"Come in the house and wash your hands."

In the kitchen as I bent over the brown earthenware sink I kept glancing across at the oven.

Mrs Butler laughed. ''Oh he's still with us. Come and have a look.''

It was difficult to see the kitten in the dark interior but when I spotted him I put out my hand and touched him and he turned his head towards me.

''He's coming round,'' I said. ''That hour in there has worked wonders.''

''Doesn't often fail.'' The farmer's wife lifted him out. ''I think he's a little tough 'un.'' She began to spoon warm milk into the tiny mouth.

''I reckon we'll have him lappin' in a day or two.''

''You're going to keep him, then?''

''Too true we are. I'm going to call him Moses.''

''*Moses?*''

''Aye, you found him among the rushes, didn't you?''

I laughed. ''That's right. It's a good name.''

I was on the Butler farm about a fortnight later
and I kept looking around for Moses.
Farmers rarely have their cats indoors and I thought
that if the black kitten had survived he would have
joined the feline colony around the buildings.

Farm cats have a pretty good time. They may
not be petted or cosseted but it has always seemed to
me that they lead a free, natural life. They are
expected to catch mice but if they are not so inclined
there is abundant food at hand; bowls of milk here
and there and the dogs' dishes to be raided if
anything interesting is left over.

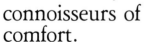I had seen plenty of cats around today,
some flitting nervously away, others friendly
and purring. There was a tabby loping gracefully
across the cobbles and a big tortoise-shell was curled
on a bed of straw at the warm
end of the byre; cats are
connoisseurs of
comfort.

When Mr Butler went to fetch some hot water I had a quick look in the bullock house and a white Tom regarded me placidly from between the bars of a hay rack where he had been taking a siesta. But there was no sign of Moses.

I finished drying my arms and was about to make a casual reference to the kitten when Mr Butler handed me my jacket.

''Come round here with me if you've got a minute,'' he said.

''I've got summat to show you.''

I followed him through the door at the end and across a passage into the long, low-roofed piggery. He stopped at a pen about half way down and pointed inside.

''Look 'ere,'' he said.

I leaned over the wall and my face must have shown my astonishment because the farmer burst into a shout of laughter.

''That's summat new for you, isn't it?''

I stared unbelievingly down at a large sow stretched comfortably on her side, suckling a litter of about twelve piglets and right in the middle of the long pink row, furry black and incongruous, was *Moses.* He had a teat in his mouth and was absorbing his nourishment with the same rapt enjoyment as his smooth-skinned fellows on either side.

''What the devil . . .?'' I gasped.

Mr Butler was still laughing. ''I thought you'd never have seen anything like that before, I never have, any road.''

''But how did it happen?'' I still couldn't drag my eyes away.

''It was the Missus's idea,'' he replied. ''When she'd got the little youth lappin' milk she took him out to find a right warm spot for him in the buildings. She settled on this pen because the sow, Bertha, had just had a litter and I had a heater in and it was grand and cosy.''

I nodded. ''Sounds just right.''

Well she put Moses and a bowl of milk in here,'' the farmer went on, ''but the little feller didn't stay by the heater very long — next time I looked in he was round at t'milk bar.''

I shrugged my shoulders. ''They say you see something new every day at this game, but this is something I've never even heard of. Anyway, he looks well on it — does he actually live on the sow's milk or does he still drink from his bowl?''

''A bit of both, I reckon. It's hard to say.''

Anyway, whatever mixture Moses was getting he grew rapidly into a sleek, handsome animal with an unusually high gloss to his coat which may or may not have been due to the porcine element of his diet.

I never went to the Butlers' without having a look in the pig pen. Bertha, his foster mother, seemed to find nothing unusual in this hairy intruder and pushed him around casually with pleased grunts just as she did with the rest of her brood.

Moses for his part appeared to find the society of the pigs very congenial. When the piglets curled up together and settled down for a sleep Moses would be somewhere in the heap and when his young colleagues were weaned at eight weeks he showed his attachment to Bertha by spending most of his time with her.

And it stayed that way over the years. Often he would be right inside the pen, rubbing himself happily along the comforting bulk of the sow, but I remember him best in his favourite place; crouching on the wall looking down perhaps meditatively on what had been his first warm home.